T0193886

GOD
THE

KIND
OF

FAITH

DUDLEY BENT

authorHOUSE®

AuthorHouse™
1663 Liberty Drive
Bloomington, IN 47403
www.authorhouse.com
Phone: 1 (800) 839-8640

© 2019 Dudley Bent. All rights reserved.

No part of this book may be reproduced, stored in a retrieval system, or transmitted by any means without the written permission of the author.

Published by AuthorHouse 10/14/2019

ISBN: 978-1-7283-3155-3 (sc)
ISBN: 978-1-7283-3154-6 (e)

Print information available on the last page.

Any people depicted in stock imagery provided by Getty Images are models, and such images are being used for illustrative purposes only. Certain stock imagery © Getty Images.

This book is printed on acid-free paper.

Because of the dynamic nature of the Internet, any web addresses or links contained in this book may have changed since publication and may no longer be valid. The views expressed in this work are solely those of the author and do not necessarily reflect the views of the publisher, and the publisher hereby disclaims any responsibility for them.

Scripture quotations marked KJV are from the Holy Bible, King James Version (Authorized Version). First published in 1611. Quoted from the KJV Classic Reference Bible, Copyright © 1983 by The Zondervan Corporation.

This book is dedicated to all those who believe
that the possible can be made possible.

Contents

FOREWORD

This isn't just another book about Christian philosophy; it's a book about the power of faith, and there is no better person to write on it than Bishop Dr. Dudley Bent Sr. In this book, Dr. Bent takes the reader through a practical and insightful journey of faith and how it has played a role in his life.

Bishop Dr. Dudley Bent Sr. has been in the ministry for over fifty years. He and his wife, Pastor Joyce Bent, established the Pentecostal Church of God (Trinity) in the South Central Ontario District and cofounded Deliverance Temple, Deliverance Miracle Centre, and Faith Worship Centre. He is the father of four children and proud grandfather of four grandchildren.

If you were to sit down and have a conversation with Bishop Bent, he would tell you that he has been living by faith his entire Christian life. The God kind of faith has enabled him to overcome many of life's challenges. Bishop Bent wants to leave a recorded legacy of his series of sermons on the topic of faith and share lessons that will engage his reader but, more importantly, allow them to see how faith can play a major role in their lives.

The first time I read *The God Kind of Faith,* I learned more about faith than I have learned from any other single source on this principle. There are power and possibilities when you strengthen your faith in God.

This book will provide insight and biblical examples of how faith has worked for others and how it can work for you. No one can read this book without having a growth experience in the most important department of your life.

Congratulations! You have opened the door to a genuine learning and growth experience that I promise will be fantastic.

Simone Jennifer Smith, founder of Hear 2 Help Community Development

Acknowledgments

So many people have influenced this book and have had a significant influence in my life and my ministry, but today, I would like to acknowledge four of them. First, I acknowledge my loving wife, Joyce, who remains my best friend and who has never failed me. She is a loving partner and companion who has always believed in me and for forty-nine years has stood beside me through the good and bad times.

Secondly, I recognize my hero, my mother, Rowener Frater-Staple, who laid the Christian foundation in my life. Although she has passed, she will never be forgotten. She is forever the wind beneath my wings.

Thirdly, I bestow great thanks to Dr. William Comfort of Chesapeake, Maryland, for his words of wisdom that have provided me with motivation and godly direction.

Finally, I want to pay tribute to Dr. Kenneth Erwin Hagin from Tulsa, Oklahoma, United States, who through his messages, books, CDs, and tapes has provided me with inspiration and many keys to the Word of God.

Introduction

The God Kind of Faith

> Have faith in God. For truly I say to you that whoever shall say to this mountain, be moved and be cast into the sea, and shall not doubt in his heart, but shall believe that what he said shall occur, he shall have whatever he said. Therefore, I say to you, all things, whatever you ask, praying, believe that you shall receive them, and it will be to you.
>
> —Mark 11:22–24

As we look out at the world today, it is easy to understand why many of us get discouraged. It is not always easy to ask people to have faith in something or someone they cannot see; however, this book is written to show people how to place their faith in God. When you read *The God Kind of Faith,* it will provide examples of how God Himself had faith, and it will teach you how to attain faith and hold on to it.

I remember when I first realized the power of having faith. I was twenty-two years old, and my desire from God was for my first home. Without having that first dollar in my pocket, my wife and I went to the Realtor and discussed with her that we were interested in buying a home. The Realtor took us to a ten-bedroom home in the heart of downtown Toronto. After my wife saw this beautiful house, she was sold, and as a doting husband, there was nothing I would not do for my wife. You know what they say: "A happy wife is a happy life." We informed the Realtor that we didn't have the finances for the home at that time, but we believed the Lord for this home. Right after our meeting, my wife and I walked around the home and claimed it by faith.

As two young newlyweds, we took that first step of faith and watched God go to work. We knew that if we believed His Word and held strong to our faith, we would have what we said. In a matter of weeks, God supplied the finances for the down payment. Our lawyer was shocked and amazed that as young people we were able to come up with the finances in such a short span of time. When we were closing the home, the lawyer asked me if I knew somebody from above. Filled with a sense of pride and humbled by the work of our God Almighty, I replied with an enthusiastic "You bet!"

This was my first taste of what it was like to stand on raw, unwavering faith—the God kind of faith—and it was the best feeling ever! It was here that I realized God doesn't need anything else from us but our faith. We just need to believe and stand firm to what His promises are so we can become possessors.

God's faith as we see in Genesis is profound. He used His words and spoke the world into existence, breathing life into the living things on earth and creating us in the image and likeness of Him. Everything in the physical realm we call earth was called into existence by the faith of God. God is calling us to believe and speak things into existence in our lives.

If we access the God kind of faith, we can achieve the impossible. All faith in God is based on the Word of God. This is because faith in God is based on the will of God, and the will of God is communicated to us by the Word of God. To understand faith itself, one must study scriptures on faith, and throughout this book, I will provide you with everything that you need to grow your faith. To become stronger in anything that you do, you must take time with it, study it, learn it, and practice it. This book will help to break down the message of the God kind of faith so you can depict its true meaning.

Never give up on your hopes and your dreams just because you faced some initial setbacks. Lean on the faith of God as often as possible, and you will soon come to realize why having unwavering faith is so important in life. For those who have recently gained a desire to learn more about faith, this book will not only provide biblical evidence of faith but also faith reflection points and faith forming scriptures written to point you in the direction to activating that God kind of faith.

Chapter 1

What is Faith?

Faith is the substance of things hoped for the evidence of things not seen.

—Hebrews 11:1

In 1975 when I was a new convert, this was one of the first scripture verses my pastor introduced to my class when he taught us about faith. It was during this time that I wrestled with this subject of faith and was drawn to obtaining a full understanding of what faith really is. I learned rather quickly in my spiritual journey that faith is the anchor to our Christian lives. Without it, we are incapable of attaining the entirety that God has for us here during our time here on earth. So the question before us is "What is faith?"

Faith is a gift from God. You are given faith by believing that Jesus is the Christ, the Son of God. Faith is absolutely essential in receiving God's blessings. It helps you to discover your purpose in life and acts as the pathway to finding solutions. If you really want something in life, faith is the thing that helps you to see that through. It is at the core of a persistent heart.

So how do you know you have this faith? How do you know you are trusting God? After fifty years of walking in faith and being established in the faith, I can unequivocally state that faith is learning to trust God and believing that God tells the truth. Faith is identified when we fully believe that God will do what He has said He will do. God speaks His truth through the Bible, revealing everything He can do in our lives. However, it is up to us to wholeheartedly believe what He has stated in His Word.

> God will avenge them speedily. Nevertheless when the Son of man cometh, shall He find faith on the earth? (Luke 18:8)

The questions here are these: Will God find what He is looking for? Will He really find those who are applying faith in their lives? When God first made man in His image, His desire was that we would have this unwavering faith that can be found in His Word. The one thing that God is looking for in your life and in my life is faith.

Why faith? Why is the Lord looking for faith and not grace, love, or hope? I am not implying that grace, love, and hope are not necessary in our walk with the Lord. Nonetheless, faith is an essential anchor to our walk. God takes pleasure in seeing us being established in our faith and living a life of faith.

> But without faith it is impossible to please him: for he that cometh to God must believe that he is, and that he is a rewarder of them that diligently seek him. (Hebrews 11:6)

This is a statement of great consequences and significance. He does not say, "Without faith it is difficult to please God." He says, "Without faith it is impossible to please God." We need to understand that the only way our lives can be pleasing to God is through faith. Consequently, that means if I am not living a life of faith, I am not pleasing the Lord. As we delve deeper into the topic of faith, we will find that God wants us to understand that whatever is not from faith is sin.

> And he that doubteth is damned if he eat, because he eateth not of faith: for whatsoever is not of faith is sin. (Romans 14:23)

This verse brings into questions our thoughts on sin. We all like the old definitions of sin: drinking is sin, dancing is sin, smoking is sin, and gambling is sin. We can pretty well handle that. But when God comes along and says, "Whatever is not of faith is sin," it sheds light on the fact that if we are not living lives of faith, we are living lives of sin.

Faith is not a luxury item that we can add if we want to; it is absolutely essential and can be viewed almost like a survival tool. The only way we can please God is by faith, and that makes it imperative that Christians know what it means to live by faith.

What Does It Mean to Live by Faith?

Most Christians seem to have the idea that faith is a mysterious gift that God gives to a few special people. People may think, *Well, I could never live that way because it is reserved for just a few super saints.* However, every believer has the capacity to live a mighty life of faith. *My faith is weak.* These are the thoughts that might be part of your reality in this moment, but I challenge you to read the gospels. You will see that every person who came to Jesus came to Him with imperfect and weak faith. Jesus honored that mustard seed faith by providing them with miracles and granting them their hearts' desires.

For too long we have allowed the devil to rob us of blessings by allowing him to convince us that our faith is weak. Although this may be true, our faith has the potential to grow and become strong enough to move mountains. It is not the size of your faith that matters. It is your willingness to exercise it and believe in God's Word.

Chapter 2

A Deeper Understanding of Faith

For I am not ashamed of the gospel of Christ for it is the power of God unto salvation to everyone that believe it, to the Jews first. For in it is the righteousness of God revealed from Faith to Faith as it is written, the just shall live by faith.

—Romans 1:16–17

What is faith? How does it work? Where does it come from? What is it for? These are some of the questions I will try to answer throughout this book.

Faith is the foundation of the Christian life, yet many believers don't fully understand what true Bible faith is. When we look into it, the faith I am speaking of is the kind of faith that spoke the universe into existence; this God kind of faith called things that are not as though they were. God said, "Let there be light," and there was light. We are created in the image of God, which means that we can do the very same thing. We too as believers can call things that are not as though they were. I believe that God wants us to understand the power we possess with faith as the source of our strength. We can call things that are not as though they were; we can create.

Faith Fact

Did you know that faith is referred to 2,045 times in the Bible? And the word *believe* is used 178 times.

Let's continue further developing our understanding of what faith is by examining its definition. Faith is defined in the first verse of the faith chapter of Hebrews 11, which states, "Now faith is the substance of things hoped for, the evidence of things not seen" (Hebrews 11:1).

The Greek word for *faith,* #4102 in *Strong's Concordance,* means "persuasion, conviction of religious truth, conviction of truthfulness of God, or reliance on God." It comes from #3982, which means to "convince, to assent to evidence or authority, or to rely on by inward certainty." We see that faith is the assurance that we will receive the things for which we hope, and it supports the knowledge that we will receive them. The Bible has promises of blessing in this life if we obey God; it also contains promises of eternal life in the kingdom of God. Faith is the assurance that we will receive those promises. It provides the evidence of what we cannot see or of what we have not seen yet. By faith, we know that God made the universe. And although we cannot see God, faith is the evidence or proof that God exists and that He will keep His promises, even though we have not seen those promises yet.

This Bible verse does not define faith in terms of our five senses—sight, hearing, touch, smell, and taste—because if we could perceive the object of our faith, we would not need faith. The evidence is in the Bible and the physical creation around us. Will we have the faith to believe this?

> Being fully convinced that what he had promised he was able to perform. (Romans 4:16–21)

Abraham believed that God would keep His promises, and he was assured that he would receive them. Abraham has what I like to call *the God kind of faith.*

Chapter 3

THE PURPOSE OF FAITH

The purpose of faith is to remove mountains. Mark wrote in the scriptures about a distinct teaching from Jesus regarding faith. He stated that Jesus said, "Have faith in God" or "Have the God kind of faith," and then say to the mountain, "Go!"

> And Jesus answering saith unto them, "Have faith in God."
>
> "For verily I say unto you, That whosoever shall say unto this mountain, Be thou removed, and be thou cast into the sea; and shall not doubt in his heart, but shall believe that those things which he saith shall come to pass; he shall have whatsoever he saith."
> "Therefore I say unto you, What things soever ye desire, when ye pray, believe that ye receive them, and ye shall have them." (Mark 11:22–24)

The mountain that Jesus was referring to is a metaphor for life's trials, tests, heartaches, pains, difficulties, finances, tribulations, sicknesses, diseases, and basically any form of testing within our lives. To successfully strengthen our faith, we need to understand how to effectively remove these mountains that will continuously pop up in life.

There are two important points to note about these scriptures: speaking words of faith and understanding the power of the Word.

Speaking Words of Faith

Speak the creative word. The creative word gives life and creates what is established in the spiritual world into your physical world. Faith talk begins with you prophetically speaking the word of the Lord in every area of your life.

> This book of the law shall not depart out of thy mouth; but thou shalt meditate therein day and night, that thou mayest observe to do according to all that is written therein: for then thou shalt make thy way prosperous, and then thou shalt have good success. (Joshua 1:8)

God informed Joshua that he could be prosperous and successful as long as the Word of the Lord did not depart from his mouth and he continued to meditate on it day and night. So it is with us; we too need to meditate and utter the Word of the Lord daily. I encourage you to confess the first set of prophetic scriptures I have listed below over your life daily and watch the changes that will materialize. It just takes some practice and dedication.

Daily Prophetic Scriptures

1. "When I resist Satan he flees from me. If I could not resist Satan, God would not have told me to do so" (James 4:7).
2. "I receive the desire of my heart when I delight myself in the Lord" (Psalm 37:4).
3. "I had faint unless I had believed to see the goodness of the Lord in the land of the living" (Psalm 27:13).
4. "By Jesus Christ, I rain as king in life" (Romans 5:17).
5. "The Lord is the strength of my life" (Psalm 27:1).
6. "I can do all things through Christ who strengthened me" (Philippians 4:13).
7. "The joy of the Lord is my strength" (Nehemiah 8:10).
8. "I quench all the fiery darts of the devil because I am cleansed by the blood of Jesus" (Revelation 12:11).

9. "I have great peace because I am taught of the Lord" (Isaiah 54:13).

Understanding the Power of the Word

The second point that needs to be addressed is our understanding of the power in words. Our mountains at times can get us distracted from what the Word of God says. Do not allow the enemy to get you distracted from your purpose or your faith. The Bible identifies that speaking the creative word will make a difference in our lives and is vitally important to our success. Here are nine dynamic scriptures that reiterate the importance of your words.

<u>The Power of the Word Scriptures</u>

1. "By my words I am justified and by my words I am condemned" (Matthew 12:34).
2. "Death and life are in the tongue" (Proverbs 18:21).
3. "I can be snared by my own words" (Proverbs 6:21)
4. "If I speak his words, then his words will not return void" (Isaiah 53:11).
5. "If I speak his words then faith cometh by his words" (Romans 10:17).
6. "If I speak his words, then he sends his words and heals" (Psalm 107:20).
7. "If I speak his words, then his words are health to all my bones" (Proverbs 4:22).
8. "If I speak his words, then the devils are cast out by his words" (Matthew 8:16).
9. "If I speak his words, then his words run very swiftly" (Psalm 147:15).

When you align your words with the Word of God, it will bring about a supernatural change in your life. The more you speak the Word of God *only,* the more you will have faith in God. The more you have faith in

God, the more you will believe in God. The more you believe in God, the more you can experience the removal of mountains in your life that are preventing you from experiencing the abundance that God wants you to experience here on earth.

Chapter 4

HOW DO WE RECEIVE FAITH?

For by grace are ye saved through faith, and that not of yourselves; it is the gift of God.

—Ephesians 2:8

Knowing how we obtain faith helps us to understand what faith is. It is not something that we just work up or find within ourselves; on the contrary, it is a gift from God. And it is not based on our works and our own efforts as Christians. Paul wrote to the Galatians,

Knowing that a man is not justified by the works of the law, but by the faith of Jesus Christ, even we have believed in Jesus Christ, that we might be justified by the faith of Christ, and not by the works of the law: for by the works of the law shall no flesh be justified. (Galatians 2:16)

Faith is the greatest part of our Christian life, and our acceptance of Jesus Christ transpires through faith. God has presented faith to man and it is up to man to accept it through Jesus Christ. As you submit your life to Christ, He will allow you to live your best life.

> I am crucified with Christ; nevertheless I live; yet not I;
> but Christ liveth in me; and the life which I now live in
> the flesh I live by the faith of the Son of God who loved
> me and gave himself for me. (Galatians 2:20)

When Jesus lived on earth as one of us, He knew that He could not accomplish anything of true value on His own.

> I can of mine own self do nothing: as I hear, I judge: and
> my judgment is just; because I seek not mine own will,
> but the will of the Father which hath sent me. (John 5:30)

Just as Jesus needed the will of the Father to successfully accomplish His purpose on earth, we too need assistance. It is difficult to do anything spiritually on our own. Thus, we need God's faith in us.

Chapter 5

Have Faith in God

Have faith in God.

—Mark 11:22

Jesus wants us to have the God kind of faith. This God kind of faith is the only thing that will move the hand of God. It is a faith that relies on the ability of God. When you have this type of faith, it becomes a persistent force that exists in your life daily. You will overcome life's tests and tribulations because the God kind of faith always overcomes. It is a faith that never argues; it never brags on itself. It is never nervous; it never trembles. The God kind of faith is never overpowered and never gets excited. This type of faith looks directly to the Word of God.

You can stand on faith knowing that what God says is a revelation of what His will is. This faith accepts God's Word as final, and it claims that Word and stands firm on it. You are then able to claim your covenanted rights as a Christian. With the God kind of faith, you become a possessor of the promises of God.

Having faith in God allows you to stand steadfast and immovable because your faith knows what God has said. Therefore, when reason argues, when one fears, trembles, and becomes nervous, it is faith that settles these emotions. To see the full potential of your faith, you must be grounded in the Word of God. You must know His Word so that you can know His will. As believers, we need to bring our requests to God and leave the results with Him. Give Him a chance to do for you what He has been waiting so long to do but could not until you were ready to act on His Word in faith.

Let's take another look at the life of Abraham. He's a great biblical example of someone who understood what it is to believe God.

> And being not weak in faith, he staggered not at the promise of God through unbelief; but was strong in faith, giving glory to God; being fully persuaded that, what he [God] had promised, he was able also to perform. (Romans 4:19–21)

God was able to perform great wonders in Abraham's life. His story is a great one to look into because it explores how faith was used in a situation that seemed impossible to man but was not impossible to God. You can read more about his journey in Genesis 12–17.

Right now I want you to go to God and present the desires of your heart. Ask Him to do it; pray the prayer of faith for that promise; place your order in faith, and turn it loose. Trust it to the heavenly authorities to take it through and to bring you the order properly filled. Don't keep praying again and again for the thing desired. Release your desire in faith, and allow God to grant you whatsoever you wish. Maintain this attitude of faith, and refuse to be moved. Let nothing budge you from your stand on the promise of God, and your prayer will be answered to the fullest extent.

> Go your way; and as you have believed, so be it done to you. (Matthew 8:13)

Chapter 6

Faith Is the Substance

> Now faith is the substance of things hoped for, the
> evidence of things not seen.
>
> —Hebrews 11:1

The word *substance* was used in the New Testament as the proof or the evidence of ownership. For instance, I might own a house, and the proof that I own the house is that I have the title deed to it. The title deed is all I need to prove I own that house. I did not necessarily have to show you the house.

The Bible says faith is the claim; it is the title deed of things hoped for. Things hoped for is another way of speaking of things that God has promised that we do not yet possess. The way the word *hope* in the Bible is used has never had an element of doubt. We at times say things like "Well, I hope this thing happens" or "I hope it doesn't rain." These types of statements leave room for doubt. There is uncertainty; there is the possibility that it might not come to pass.

When using a biblical approach with the word *hope*, there is no element of doubt that exists. Hope is the absolute assurance that what God promised will come to pass. The word *hope* is used because we do not yet possess it; it is now viewed as a confident expectation. Faith is my title deed, my proof of ownership, my proof of those things God has promised that I am not yet in possession of, etc. Faith enables me to have what God has promised, and it becomes the reality of things that I confidently hope for.

God has never asked anyone to believe Him for anything that He has not promised to do. Here is a list of God's promises and blessings that you can confess over your life. Use your faith, and claim what God has declared in His Word as yours.

Scriptures on Blessings

1. Blessings on obedience (Deuteronomy 28:1–11).
2. "But thou shalt remember the Lord thy God: for it is he that giveth thee power to get wealth, that he may establish his covenant which he sware unto thy fathers, as it is this day" (Deuteronomy 8:18).
3. "Christ hath redeemed us from the curse of the law, being made a curse for us: for it is written, Cursed is every one that hangeth on a tree" (Galatians 3:13).
4. "That the blessing of Abraham might come on the Gentiles through Jesus Christ; that we might receive the promise of the Spirit through faith" (Galatians 3:13–14).
5. "Therefore it is of faith, that it might be by grace; to the end the promise might be sure to all the seed; not to that only which is of the law, but to that also which is of the faith of Abraham; who is the father of us all" (Romans 4:16).
6. "And I will make of thee a great nation, and I will bless thee, and make thy name great; and thou shalt be a blessing" (Genesis 12:2).
7. "And I will bless them that bless thee, and curse him that curseth thee: and in thee shall all families of the earth be blessed" (Genesis 12:2–3).
8. "And in thy seed shall all the nations of the earth be blessed; because thou hast obeyed my voice" (Genesis 22:18).
9. "If you can believe, all things are possible to them that believe" (Mark 9:23).

Chapter 7

YOU HAVE A MEASURE OF FAITH

> I say, through the grace given to me, to everyone who is among you, not to think of himself more highly than he ought to think, but to think soberly, as God has dealt to everyone a measure of faith.
>
> —Romans 12:3–4

Some people say that we use faith all the time and even provide the example of sitting on a chair as an exercise of our faith. However, this is not real Bible faith. Bible faith has a spiritual dimension because it comes as a direct result of the activity of God. God has given each of us a measure of faith, but that doesn't mean that's all we can have. Your faith can be increased.

> Not boasting of things beyond measure, that is, in other men's labours, but having hope, that as your faith is increase, we shall be greatly enlarged by you in our sphere. (Corinthians 10:15)

Paul would not be saying that if it were not possible to increase our faith. It is a gift, and we must remain humble in receiving. For I say, through the grace given to you, to disengage from ego and to not think of yourself more highly than you ought to think but to think soberly.

> For who maketh thee to differ from another? and what hast thou that thou didst not receive? now if thou didst receive it, why dost thou glory, as if thou hadst not received it? (1 Corinthians 4:7)

Being proud of the amount of faith you have is like being proud of your good looks. You cannot help being good-looking, tall, intelligent, talented, or anything else. We were all born with different strengths and abilities, and we all have different measures of faith. I could never fill your shoes because I wasn't given the measure of faith you were given.

> For I say, through the grace given unto me, to every man that is among you, not to think of himself more highly than he ought to think; but to think soberly, according as God hath dealt to every man the measure of faith. (Romans 12:3)

Here God is stating that every person has a "measure" or has a certain amount of faith. As a result, there cannot be any excuse of not having faith to advance your life or to overcome difficulties within your life. You may say my faith is little; however, do not forget what Jesus said about the grain of a mustard seed.

> Even if your faith is the grain of a mustard seed you can use it to move life's mountains and cause the impossible to come to pass. (Matthew 17:20)

Let's take, for instance, how you accepted salvation. How did you get saved? You heard the Word preached and believed the preacher was speaking the truth concerning the Word of God. You received salvation by hearing the Word of God, believing it, and confessing you were saved.

> Because faith cometh by hearing and hearing the word of Jesus. (Romans 10:17)

Your measure of faith can make the impossible possible. Let's look at how Jesus effectively used His measure of faith when He spoke to the fig tree and cursed it. Jesus understood that there is power in the spoken word. His intention was not just to curse the fig tree but to teach His disciples about how to use their faith.

Peter, being one of Jesus's followers, immediately identified that what Jesus had spoken about the fig tree had come to pass.

> And Peter calling to remembrance saith unto him, Master, behold, the fig tree which thou cursedst is withered away. (Mark 11:21)

Peter was astonished, and his words seem to indicate that he thought Jesus would be surprised also. However, notice Jesus's answer was very calm and very deliberate. "And Jesus answering saith unto them, Have faith in God." Jesus was telling Peter to not get excited about a little fig tree being withered. Drying up the fig tree was nothing. Instead Jesus confirmed to Peter that if you have faith in God, you will do more than wither fig trees. You can say to mountains, "Get out of the way," and they will have to get out of the way.

Jesus understood how to effectively use the creative word, combined with his measure of faith by calling things that are not as though they were. In this situation, Jesus demonstrated to His disciples that if they can just believe, then all things are possible.

In many other texts, mountains symbolize barriers, obstacles, and enemies. What our Lord is saying is that if you have faith in God and you follow Him, believe in Him, and are committed to do

His will, you will come to a mountain that is blocking your path and boldly say to the mountain, "Get out of the way," and it shall move.

I want to encourage everyone not to be afraid to activate their measure of faith. I dare you to take the first step of faith and watch what God will do in and through your life. If you will put your faith to work, no mountain will be able to stand before you.

> Every place the sole of your foot shall thread upon I have given it to you. (Joshua 1:3)

Chapter 8

Benefits of Faith

When you have faith in God, God unleashes benefits into your life. What are these benefits that God releases? As you read through the Bible, there are numerous scriptures that identify what is in store for us when we use our faith.

> What things so ever ye desire, when ye pray, believe that
> ye receive them, and ye shall have them. (Mark 11:24)

When you activate your faith and remain steadfast on what you believe, Jesus declares you will receive those things you desire.

Faith Reflection Moment

What are you praying about?

What do you believe?

Take a moment to think about the reflection questions presented. Our faith is the gateway that provides an avenue for God to respond to our prayers. It is through faith that our prayers about any situation, obstacle, tribulation, heartache, sickness, and decision are answered.

During Jesus's time on earth, He made it His focus to illustrate just how easy it is to unfold the benefits of faith.

> Then he touched their eyes, saying, according to your faith be it unto you. (Matthew 9:29)

In this situation, both men experienced healing and became free from blindness based solely upon their individual faith. It was their faith that caused Jesus to move and heal their eyes. We as Christians must see the vital importance of faith in our Christian journey. Jesus sums it up rather well.

> If thou canst believe, all things are possible to him that believeth. (Mark 9:23)

As you use your faith, not only can you move obstacles and cause positive changes in your life, but more importantly, *nothing* will be impossible for you to attain because you have faith in God.

Let's take a moment to discuss the idea of patience and how it relates to faith. It is imperative in our understanding of faith to be aware that God might not answer our prayer immediately. If He did, we would not need faith for very long.

> My brethren, count it all joy when ye fall into divers temptations; Knowing this, that the trying of your faith worketh patience. (James 1:2–3)

When our faith is tested by not receiving our desires right away, patience is the result. James further states,

> But let patience have her perfect work, that ye may be perfect and entire, wanting nothing. If any of you lack wisdom, let him ask of God, that giveth to all men liberally, and unbraideth not; and it shall be given to him. (James 1:4)

We must let God work with us to produce His perfect character in us, which is a benefit of faith. Below I have listed scriptures that outline the benefits of faith in different areas of your life. Review these, and reflect on them.

Benefits of Faith Scriptures

1. Faith brings all the benefits of salvation into our lives (Ephesians 2:8–9).
2. Faith brings eternal life (John 3:16).
3. Faith brings no judgment, but you will pass from death to life (John 5:24).
4. Faith brings answers to prayers (Matthew 21:22).
5. Faith brings material provision (Matthew 6:11).
6. Faith brings healing, prosperity, peace, love, and joy (1 Peter 1:8; Isaiah 53:5).
7. Faith brings healing and deliverance to your ministry (Mark 9:23; Mark 10:52; James 5:13-16).
8. Faith makes the impossible possible (Matthew 17:20).

Chapter 9

Grace Through Faith

As you have therefore received Christ Jesus the Lord, so walk in Him.

—Colossians 2:6

In writing to the Colossians, Paul said the way that you received Him is the way that you walk in Him. You received Him by grace through faith. Everything that you and I receive in this Christian life is by grace through faith. All of salvation is by grace through faith, which means that you cannot be saved one way and live another way. You do not begin in the spirit and then are made perfect in the flesh.

> Even when we were dead in trespasses, made us alive together with Christ (by grace you have been saved) … For by grace you have been saved through faith, and that not of yourselves; is it the gift of God. (Ephesians 2:5, 8)

There is a reciprocal relationship occurring with God's grace and man's faith. God gives grace, and men must act on faith. Grace grants favor and make all things possible. All we have to do as Christians is accept it. We must understand that grace makes everything possible, and it is by faith that we bring it into our experience. Faith is the hand of man that reaches out to take what God is offering Him. Take some time to review these grace scriptures as they will reveal how grace and faith correlate.

Grace Scriptures

1. Faith in Christ brings us into a new relationship with God (Romans 3:22-24; Romans 1:18; 8:1; Ephesians 2:8-9; Titus 2:11-12).
2. Grace is being given what we do not deserve. (1 Corinthians 15:10; 1 Timothy 9-16).
3. God gives grace to believers to be "made free from sin" (Romans 6:20, 22; Romans 5:20).
4. God's grace is sufficient (2 Corinthians 12:9).
5. God has given us a measure of grace as a gift (Ephesians 4:7; 1 Corinthians 1:4).
6. Read Abraham's journey as it relates to grace and faith (Romans 4:1-25).

CHAPTER 10

FAITH DISPELS FEAR

Faith is much more powerful than fear, just as light is more powerful than darkness. The opposite of faith is fear; they quite literally appear on opposite ends of a spectrum. When we look at fear, we must understand that fear is faith in the ability of Satan. Here, Satan uses fear to bring to fruition all the things we do not want in our lives. Where there is fear, there is no faith. You cannot experience fear and faith simultaneously. Either you have faith or you have fear.

Faith Reflection Moment

What do you believe?

What is heightening fear in your life?

In what areas in your life are you able to practice your faith without feeling fear?

When you exist in the realm of fear, you cannot expect to see God move on your behalf because God only moves when we are in faith. Faith produces faith. Fear produces fear. Faith and fear do not intermingle.

God's first words spoken in Genesis, "Let there be," identifies the creative power that exists in His words. Today, His words still have creative power; I can program my spirit with His Word. When I submit myself to God, I am submitting myself to His Word. Conversely, when there is no word, there is no faith.

Below are some reflective scriptures that focus on the power of words. Take a moment to review these scriptures.

The Power of Words Scriptures

1. "I live by every word that proceeds out of the mouth of God" (Matthew 4:7).
2. "My words can either create good or evil. Faith is absent when the word is absent" (Romans 10:17).
3. "I will fill my heart (spirit) full of God's word, for out of the abundance of my heart my mouth speaks" (Matthew 12:34).

Words are first conceived in our hearts, and then they are formed in our mouths. These words that are formed from our mouths may release the power of God or of Satan.

Take another moment to reflect on the questions below; the goal is not to be perfect but to practice perfection.

Faith Reflection Moment

What words are you releasing from your mouth?

Are they the words of the Lord (i.e., positive, uplifting, motivation, and/or inspirational)?

Are they the words of Satan (i.e., negative, degrading, gossip, and/or words of lack)?

A great way to remain in awareness of our words is by reading the Bible. We must refuse to establish Satan's word. The pressures of life will cause what is in our hearts to come out, whether it is God's Word or Satan's word. What is in your spirit will come out of your mouth and create good or evil. The wrong confession comes from the heart and defiles the mouth. This wrong confession may cause murder, theft, blasphemy, and lack.

If you find yourself experiencing fear in any area of your life, I want to leave with you the following scriptures. They will help to alleviate all fears in your life and strengthen your faith in the Lord.

Dismissing Fear Scriptures

1. And the LORD, he it is that doth go before thee; he will be with thee, he will not fail thee, neither forsake thee: fear not, neither be dismayed (Deuteronomy 31:8).
2. Be strong and courageous. Do not be afraid or terrified because of them, for the Lord your God goes with you; he will never leave you nor forsake you (Deuteronomy 31:6).
3. The Lord is my rock, and my fortress, and my deliverer; my God, my strength, in whom I will trust; my buckler, and the horn of my salvation, and my high tower (Psalm 18:2).
4. Even though I walk through the valley of the shadow of death, I will fear no evil, for you are with me; your rod and your staff, they comfort me (Psalm 23:4).
5. The Lord is my light and my salvation—whom shall I fear? The Lord is the stronghold of my life—of whom shall I be afraid (Psalm 27:1)?
6. I prayed to the Lord, and he answered me. He freed me from all my fears (Psalm 34:4).
7. When I am afraid, I put my trust in you (Psalm 56:3).
8. When anxiety was great within me, your consolation brought joy to my soul (Psalm 94:19).
9. So do not fear, for I am with you; do not be dismayed, for I am your God. I will strengthen you and help you; I will uphold you with my righteous right hand (Isaiah 41:10).
10. But now, this is what the Lord says ... Fear not, for I have redeemed you; I have summoned you by name; you are mine (Isaiah 43:1).

11. Peace is what I leave with you; it is my own peace that I give you I do not give it as the world does. Do not be worried and upset; do not be afraid (John 14:27).

12. And I am convinced that nothing can ever separate us from God's love. Neither death nor life, neither angels nor demons, neither our fears for today nor our worries about tomorrow—not even the powers of hell can separate us from God's love (Romans 8:38–39).

13. Do not be anxious about anything, but in every situation, by prayer and petition, with thanksgiving, present your requests to God. And the peace of God, which transcends all understanding, will guard your hearts and your minds in Christ Jesus (Philippians 4:6–7).

14. For God has not given us a spirit of fear, but of power and of love and of a sound mind (2 Timothy 1:7).

15. There is no fear in love. But perfect love drives out fear, because fear has to do with punishment. The one who fears is not made perfect in love (1 John 4:18).

Chapter 11

DON'T LET YOUR EMOTIONS TRICK YOU!

It is imperative that we have a firm understanding of how our feelings and our faith interact. Feelings bring about a variety of emotions, such as embarrassment, happiness, anger, and sadness. Feelings are sensitive, inconsistent, unregulated, vague, irrational, and an uncontrolled emotional state. Faith cannot operate under the same conditions that feelings do; faith is concrete, is emotionless, and does not waver.

It is important to note that one of our human emotions is ordinary hope. This hope does not equate to faith due to its reliance on our emotions. The hope I refer to here is the everyday human emotion that does not have a basis for expectancy. Many people mistake hope for faith. People will make statements like "I hope I get healed," "I hope I will be better, "I hope I am saved," and the ever popular "I hope God answers my prayers." The empty human emotion of hope is never faith. Ordinary hope wants something to happen or be true. This type of hope focuses on the idea that what one cherishes or desires will be fulfilled. However, the main shortfall of ordinary hope is that there is no foundation that anchors what an individual is hoping for. Ordinary hope has no basis for expecting fulfillment. Conversely, there is a biblical hope, a spiritual hope, that is anchored in Christ. With this hope, Christians can be confident in what God has promised for them.

However, if we act according to our feelings or judge things based upon our current experiences, we will never know the blessings of God's power. When our feelings attempt to override our faith, we will begin to feel weak and doubt can creep in. When we feel weak in our own flesh and confess our weakness, we glorify the adversary, who delights in tearing down our strength and blocking God's miracle power in our lives.

This is when we must use the power of God's word. If we testify according to God's Word and we are persistent in declaring, "When I am weak then I am strong," then our confession of the word will defeat our sense of weakness and our strength will be renewed. We must glorify God, who alone is able to transform our weakness into His strength, bringing victory out of defeat.

Chapter 12

FAITH CANNOT BE DENIED

When you really think about it, faith cannot be denied. What do I mean by this? When we walk in faith, believing and trusting God for the impossible and remaining steadfast in His Word, God will *always* bring your desires into fruition. The impossible will always become possible. The trials or tribulations come to an end, and more importantly, you have learned to be patient and overcome. The no in your life becomes a resounding yes! You begin to win those battles that present themselves in your Christian journey. You can walk in assurance while knowing that when you have faith, God will be pleased and be moved to honor your faith.

I thought a great way to close this book would be to provide you with examples of people in the Bible who showed unwavering faith and, because of this, their prayers were answered.

In Matthew 15:22–28, there was a woman who sought mercy form the Lord for her daughter, who was lying at home grievously vexed with a devil. Jesus took note of her persistence and unwavering faith and responded, "O woman, great is thy faith: be it unto thee even as thou wilt" (Matthew 15:28).

Her daughter was made whole from that very hour. Jesus was able to move immediately because He identified her unwavering faith and honored her faith.

Can you recall the woman who had an issue of blood for twelve years? She pressed through the crowd while speaking inwardly, "If I may touch but your clothes, I shall be made whole" (Mark 5:28).

Jesus said,

> Daughter, your faith has made you whole; go in peace and
> be whole of your plague. (Mark 5:34)

We can also look to the blind man in Mark 10. Jesus said,

> Go your way; your faith has made you whole. (Mark
> 10:52)

We can take a look at the leper who returned to give thanks. Jesus said,

> And he said unto him, Arise, go thy way: thy faith hath
> made thee whole." (Luke 17:19)

Or how about when a certain man asked Jesus to come to his house and heal his son because he was at the point of death? Jesus said to him, "Go your way, your son lives." The Bible says the man believed the word that Jesus had spoken to him, and he went on his way. While on his way home, his servants met him and declared,

> Your son lives. (John 4:47–53)

Another powerful, clear example of faith honored is when Paul was preaching the gospel at Listra. One of his hearers was a man who had been born with a defect that left him crippled. Paul waited until the lame man had heard the Word of God; he could have rushed ahead and tried to heal him, but Paul knew that the man had to truly believe and have faith. In Romans 10:17, Paul, perceiving that the man had faith to be healed, said with a loud voice, "Stand up right on your feet." And just like that, the man leaped and began to walk (See Acts 14:9–10).

Some other wonders of faith to reflect on are examples of the man with the withered hand (Matthew 12:10, 13), the man by the pool at Bethesda (John 5:5–9), the multitudes (Matthew 12:15; 14:14, 35–36), and the woman with an infirmity spirit (Luke 13:1–13).

Throughout my ministry across the globe, I have seen people who were suffering from disease and sicknesses receive their healing while listening to the message being preached.

> By faith the people of God obtain a good report. (Hebrews 11:2)

When we look to the scriptures, we see the power of faith. We see that God honors our faith as long as we trust and believe. It is our faith that causes changes in our life situations and results in us experiencing supernatural results that we saw as inconceivable. Without faith, it is impossible to experience the hand of God moving in your situation. The only way to build our faith is by practicing, so do not hesitate to pick up this book a few times a day, especially when you are feeling weary.

Remember that you are not alone and that God walks with you.

Printed in the United States
By Bookmasters